Philosophy of the Social Sciences

Study of logic and methods of the social sciences which aims to provide an interpretation of the social sciences.

A. Central Questions Of Study

1. What is the criteria of a good social explanation?
2. How are the social sciences distinct from natural sciences?
3. Is there a distinctive method for social research?
4. What are the procedures needed to evaluate social sciences assertions?
5. Are there irreducible social laws?
6. Are there causal relations among social phenomena?
7. Do social facts require reduction to facts about individuals?
8. What is the role of theory in social explanation?

B. Methods of Study

1. **Descriptive**
   a. Explanations, methods, empirical arguments, theories, hypotheses in social science literature.
   b. Philosopher needs extensive knowledge of areas of social science research.
   c. Philosopher formulates analysis of the social sciences.
   d. Philosopher's analysis corresponds to scientists' practice.
2. **Prescriptive**
   a. Field is epistemic.
   b. Concerned with scientific theories/hypotheses put forward as true or probable.
   c. Theories are justified on rational grounds.
   d. Philosopher provides critical evaluation of existing social science methods and practices.
   e. Philosopher determines if methods are true or false.
3. **Descriptive and Prescriptive Methods**
   a. Suggest philosophy of social science be construed as rational reconstruction of existing social science practice.
   b. Suggest reconstruction guided by existing practice.
   c. Suggest reconstruction extending beyond existing practice.
   d. Identify faulty assumptions, forms of reasoning, and explanatory frameworks.

C. Positions in Social Science

1. ***Naturalism*****:** Methods of the social sciences should correspond closely to natural sciences.
2. ***Physicalism*****:** All higher-level phenomena and regularities reducible to:
   a. Physical entities.
   b. Laws that govern them.
3. ***Anti-Naturalism*****:** Social sciences are inherently distinct from the natural sciences:
   a. Social phenomena are metaphysically distinguishable from natural phenomena.
   b. Social phenomena are intentional.
      i. Social phenomena depend on the meaningful actions of individuals.
      ii. Natural phenomena admit of causal explanation.
      iii. Social phenomena require intentional explanation.
      iv. Corresponding difference between the methods of natural and social science

D. Verstehen Method: *A method of intuitive interpretation of human action radically distinct from methods of inquiry in natural sciences.*

E. Interpretive Sociology: *School within the philosophy of social science that says human action is meaningless.*

1. Goal of social inquiry is to provide interpretations of human conduct within context of culturally specific arrangements.
2. Analogy between literary texts and social phenomena:
   a. Both are complex systems of meaningful elements.
   b. Goal of the interpreter is to provide an interpretation of the elements.
   c. This respect social science involves a hermeneutic inquiry.
   d. Interpreter should tease out the meanings underlying a particular complex of social behavior.
   e. Interpreter is like a literary critic composing complex literary text.
3. **Max Weber:** Relation between capitalism and the Protestant ethic.
   a. Identifies elements of western European culture that shaped human action in this environment to produce capitalism.
   b. Calvinism and capitalism are historically specific complexes of values and meanings, and
   c. We can better understand the emergence of capitalism by seeing how it corresponds to structures of Calvinism.

4. **Interpretive sociologists** take meaningfulness of social phenomena.
5. Social phenomena do not admit of causal explanation.
6. Social phenomena derive from purposive actions of individuals.

F. Causal Explanation: *Necessary to distinguish between causal relation between two events and causal determination through strict laws of nature.*

1. Social phenomena rarely derive from strict laws of nature:
   EXAMPLE: Wars do not result from antecedent political tensions in the way that earthquakes result from antecedent conditions in plate tectonics.
2. Non-deterministic causal relations derive from choices of individual persons.
3. Social phenomena admit of causal explanation.
4. Much social explanation depends on asserting causal relations between social events and processes:
   EXAMPLE: Claim that the administrative competence of the state is a crucial causal factor in determining the success or failure of a revolutionary movement.
5. Causal explanation discovers conditions existing prior to the event:
   a. Given the law-governed regularities.
   b. Sufficient to produce this event.
   EXAMPLE: To say that C is a cause of E is to assert that the occurrence of C, in the context of a field of social processes and mechanisms F, brought about E (or increased the likelihood of the occurrence of E).
6. **Causal mechanism:** A series of events or actions leading from cause to effect. EXAMPLE: Extension of trolley line from central city to periphery causes deterioration of public schools in central city. To make such claim it is necessary to provide account of social and political mechanisms that join antecedent condition to consequent.

G. Materialist Explanation: *Important variety of causal explanation in social science.*

1. Attempts to explain a social feature in terms of features of the **material environment**.
2. Explains in context in which social phenomenon occurs.
3. Features of environment include **topography** and **climate**:
   EXAMPLE: Banditry thrives in remote regions because rugged terrain makes it difficult for state to repress bandits.
4. Refers to the material needs of society – produce goods to support the population.
5. **Karl Marx**: Development of technology drives the development of property relations and political systems
6. Refers to fact of human agency in order to carry out explanation - human beings capable of making deliberative choices on basis wants and beliefs.
7. Accept that social phenomena depend on the purposive actions of individuals.

NOTE TO STUDENT: This **QUICKSTUDY®** guide is **an annotated outline of the major topics** taught in introductory Political Science courses. Due to its condensed format, use it as a Political Science guide, but not as a replacement for assigned class work.

ISBN-13: 978-157222692-0
ISBN-10: 157222692-7
9 781572 226920 50495

Relations between Social Regularities & Facts about Individuals

A. Methodological Individualism

1. Position that asserts primacy of facts about individuals over facts about social entities.
2. **Three forms**:
   a. Claim about social entities - **social entities** are reducible to ensembles of individuals: EXAMPLE: Insurance company reduced to ensemble of employees, supervisors, managers and owners whose actions constitute the company.
   b. Claim about **social concepts** - must be reducible to concepts involving only individuals:
   EXAMPLE: Concept of social class defined in terms of concepts pertaining only to individuals and their behavior.
3. Claim about **social regularities** - Must be derivable from regularities of individual behavior.

B. Methodological Holism

Social entities, facts, and laws autonomous and irreducible: EXAMPLE: Social structures such as states have dynamic properties, independent beliefs and purposes of particular persons who occupy positions within structure.

C. Micro-Foundations

Account of circumstances at the individual level that led individuals to bring about observed social regularities: EXAMPLE: Industrial strike is successful over extended period of time. Cannot explain circumstance by referring to members of union. Need information about circumstances of individual union member.

1. Social explanations not couched in non-social concepts.
2. Circumstances of individual agents may be characterized in social terms.

D. Laws of Explanation

Explanation depends on general laws governing phenomena in question: EXAMPLE: Discovery of the laws of electrodynamics permitted explanation of electromagnetic phenomena.

1. Social phenomena derive from actions of purposive men and women.
2. What kinds of regularities are available to provide social explanations?
3. Research framework formed around idea people are rational.
4. Explain behavior as outcome of achieving individual ends.
5. Set of regularities about individual behavior used as social explanation.
6. Explain complex social phenomenon as result of actions of large number of individual agent:
   a. With hypothesized set of goals.
   b. Within structured environment of choice.

F. Functional Explanations

1. Explains presence and persistence of feature in terms of beneficial consequences feature has for social system: EXAMPLE: Sports clubs in working-class Britain exist to give working-class people a way of expending energy that would otherwise go into struggles against an exploitative system, thus undermining social stability.
   a. Phenomena explained in terms of contribution to social stability.
   b. Type of explanation based on analogy between biology and sociology.
   c. Biologists explain species traits in terms of contribution to reproductive fitness.
   d. Sociologists explain social traits in terms of contribution to "social" fitness.
   e. General mechanism establishing functionality in biological realm not present in social realm: EXAMPLE: Mechanism of natural selection through which species arrives at traits locally optimal.
   f. No analogous process (natural selection) at work in the social realm.
   g. Groundless to suppose social traits exist because of beneficial consequences for good of society.
   h. Social phenomena must be buttressed by accounts of causal processes underlying functional relationships.

BarCharts,Inc.®
WORLD'S #1 ACADEMIC OUTLINE
Quick Study® ACADEMIC

POLITICAL SCIENCE

A Guide to World Politics

Theories of World Politics

A. Theory: An intellectual tool that allows us to make sense of the complex world.

1. Based on a set of core assumptions, theory paints a picture of the world, explaining how it is put together, what dangers exist and what opportunities are present.
   a. Theory may explain international behavior and/or make predictions about the future.
   b. Various theories compete to most accurately explain world politics and guide states in their international behavior.
2. **Paradigm**: When one theory is adopted by most observers as the most powerful.

Thucydides

B. Realism: A theory popularized by Greek historian Thucydides in the fifth century B.C. as a result of his analysis of the Peloponnesian War (431-404 B.C.). The theory has dominated world politics for 2,500 years.

1. **Key assumptions:**
   a. Individuals are evil by nature. The self-interest of individuals makes genuine cooperation problematic.
   b. States are guided by a national interest that dictates increased power.
   c. The international system is **anarchic**, meaning there is no supranational force capable of regulating the actions of states.
   d. Peace is obtained when states form alliances of rough equals, establishing a **balance of power**.
2. **Important concepts:**
   a. **Zero-sum game:** When the gains of one actor result in equal losses for another. Realists believe that the zero-sum nature of world politics prevents cooperation among states.
   b. **Security dilemma:** When the attempt by one state to increase its security by building up arms results in the decreased security of another state. The other state then builds up arms to increase its security.
   c. **Arms races:** The logical product of the security dilemma, when two or more states build-up their militaries in response to one another.
3. **Policy prescription:**
   a. Increase military arms to deter attack.
   b. Form alliances with other states to promote a balance of power.
   c. Be suspicious of all states, including allies, and put little faith in international organizations and international law to protect the state from attack.

C. Liberalism: A theory associated with French Enlightenment thinkers that challenges the core assumptions of realism.

1. Key assumptions:
   a. Individuals are good by nature. The fundamental concern for the welfare of others makes progress through cooperation possible.
   b. States with democratic institutions preserve peace; states with non-democratic institutions promote war.
   c. The anarchic nature of the international system can be reduced or eradicated through the establishment of effective international organizations and international law.
   d. War is not inevitable.
2. Important concepts:
   a. **Mutual benefit games:** When gains may be achieved simultaneously by more than one actor. Idealists believe that the mutual benefit nature of world politics promotes cooperation among states.
   b. **Interdependence:** A situation whereby actions and events in one state, society, or part of the world affect peoples elsewhere. According to **idealism**, interdependence promotes communication and understanding, resulting in a reduction of hostilities and war.

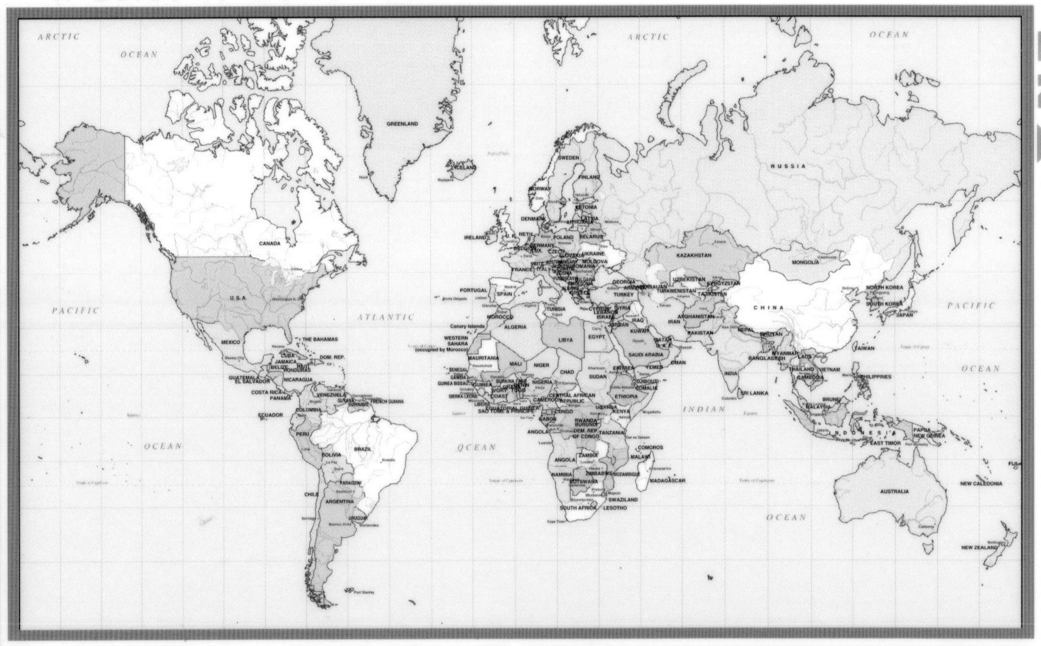

   c. **Democratic Peace**: Theory that, because democratic states do not fight each other, the spread of democratic governance throughout the world will reduce the probability of war.
3. Policy prescription:
   a. Promote democratic institutions at home and abroad.
   b. Establish and support international organizations and international law.
   c. Create links among people and states through international trade and cooperation. Reduce military arms to the level of self-defense.

D. Marxism is a theory associated with the writings of Karl Marx (1818-1883) and influential theorists such as **John Hobson** and **Vladimir Lenin**.

Karl Marx

Vladimir Lenin

1. Key assumptions:
   a. Capitalism creates two classes of people: Owners (bourgeoisie) and workers (proletariat).
   b. Owners exploit their workers in order to realize profits.
   c. The search for new markets, resources and profits leads to imperialism, the establishment of colonies outside the state.
   d. Imperialism leads to war among capitalist states.
2. Important concepts:
   a. **Class struggle:** The inevitable clash of interests between proletariat and bourgeoisie classes.
   b. **Workers' revolution:** Revolt by the proletariat against the bourgeoisie aimed at ending capitalism and introducing communism.
   c. **Communism:** An economic system in which classes are abolished and the state withers away. Under communism, each person works maximally according to ability and receives the fruits of collective labors in accordance with needs.
3. Policy prescriptions:
   a. Struggle against capitalist states in order to deter the expansion of capitalist markets.
   b. Reject international organizations and international law as tools controlled and used by capitalists to promote the interests of the bourgeoisie.

Three Levels of Analysis

A way to organize thinking about and analysis of world politics. Each level, or point of focus, illuminates some aspect of international relations. Levels of analysis help us to be systematic in our approach to understanding world politics. In examining a particular war, for example, we may identify possible causes as a characteristic of individuals, states or the international system.

A. Individual: The focus is on the key decision-makers of states. Characteristics of the individual, ranging from world view to personality profile, are examined in order to understand why a decision maker opted for a particular policy.

B. State: Characteristics associated with the state are analyzed to explain state behavior. Key state level attributes include the type of government, level of economic development and geo-strategic location.

C. International: The distribution of power among states is examined to explain events, such as world wars or imperialism. Various international structures can be identified, depending on the distribution of power. Some include:

1. **Unipolarity:** The existence of an exceptionally powerful state, or hegemon, that is both able and willing to manage the international system. Examples of hegemons include:
   a. Spain (1560-1609)
   b. France (1650-1713, 1792-1815)
   c. Great Britain (1815-1914)
   d. United States (1991-)
2. **Bipolarity:** The existence of two, roughly equal, powerful states. The cold war era (1945-1989) is exemplary of a bipolar system.
3. **Multipolarity:** When three or more great powers are identifiable. Most of modern history (1500-) has been categorized as multipolar.

***British Empire** (all years)*

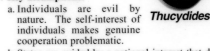

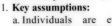

Modern International System (1500-)

A. Holy Roman Empire (1500-1648): The era is marked by the rise of the modern territorial state within the boundaries of the Holy Roman Empire, replacing the decentralized city-states, fiefdoms and princely states. The era is also characterized by the influential role of the Pope and Catholic Church.

B. Westphalian Era (1648-1815): Decentralized era following the Thirty Years' War (1618-1648) in which nation-states gained sovereign equality. The era marked the birth of international law and monopolized the legitimized use of force in the hands of governments.

C. Congress of Vienna (1815-1914): Post-Napoleonic Campaign era characterized by the Concert of Europe, which was designed to promote stability through great power negotiation of disputes.

D. Inter-War Era (1919-1939)

1. **Period after World War I** in which the international community attempted to rebound from the devastation of the war.

2. **Status quo states,** such as France and England, attempted to preserve the international system along the 1919 order.

3. **Revisionist states,** such as Germany, Japan and Italy, sought opportunities to reorder the international system in ways that would reflect their relative power and status.

4. Less involved states, such as the Soviet Union and the United States, tacitly supported the status quo states, but did not actively resist the revisionist states.

5. **The League of Nations (LON)** was established to promote international peace and security, disarmament was envisioned and international trade was promoted.

 a. The entry of Germany into the League of Nations (1926) and the drafting of the Kellogg-Briand Pact (1928), which renounced the first use of force, were high water marks of the era.

 b. The Great Depression (1929), the rearmament of Germany and the rise of Adolf Hitler (1933) eroded confidence in the ability of the world to avoid another catastrophic war. The era ended with the Germany invasion of Poland on September 1, 1939.

E. Cold War (1945-1989): Period following World War II in which the United States and the Soviet Union engaged in a global struggle for security and supremacy. Emerging from the ashes of the war as the only complete powers, the superpowers consolidated power in their respective spheres of influence, engaged in a nuclear arms race, constructed military alliances and sought allies in Third World regions. On three occasions, the two faced off in a superpower crisis.

1. **Berlin Crisis (1948):** Attempting to force West Berlin to succumb, the Soviet Union imposed a land blockade on food, energy, medicine and supplies into the pro-Western half of the city. The United States responded with an airlift that kept the West Berlin population alive until Moscow allowed supplies to reach the city.

2. **Cuban Missile Crisis (1962)**

 a. In response to intelligence reports that the Soviet Union was in the process of constructing nuclear-capable missile silos in Cuba, the Kennedy administration quarantined the Caribbean island to force the Soviets to back down.

 b. After much tension, Moscow announced that it would dismantle the silos and promise not to attempt again to place nuclear weapons in Cuba.

 c. The United States pledges not to invade Cuba and agreed to remove American missiles in Turkey in exchange.

3. **Middle East Crisis (1973)**

 a. Following the Israeli rout of Soviet-supplied Egyptian and Syrian forces during the October War, the Soviet Union announced its intention to unilaterally provide 'peacekeepers' to disengage Israeli and Egyptian forces.

 b. President Nixon placed U.S. strategic forces on an intermediate defense condition (DEFCON), escalating the crisis to the nuclear level.

 c. The Soviet Union backed down from the crisis.

F. Post-Cold War (1989-): Era characterized by American hegemony, globalization, democratization and ethnic conflict.

International Law

The rules that regulate the relations of states with other states, international organizations and individuals are called International Law. Modern international law was born in 1648 when the decline of the Catholic Church in Europe required states to regulate themselves through the establishment of international laws.

A. Primary Sources of International Law

1. **Treaty:** Explicit, written agreement between states that regulates their behavior. Once established, treaty law is binding upon all states that have ratified the treaty.

 a. Steps in the creation of a treaty:

  i. **Drafting:** Representatives of states negotiate the text of the treaty.

  ii. **Adoption:** Representatives sign the treaty text, indicating approval.

  iii. **Ratification:** Endorsement by the governmental branch empowered to ratify treaties.

  iv. **Entry into force:** When a specified number of states have ratified the treaty, it becomes binding international law.

2. Ways to change or terminate a treaty:

 a. **Expiration:** The treaty's stated duration expires.

 b. **Amendment:** A negotiated alteration of an existing treaty.

 c. **Impossibility of performance:** When behavior required by a treaty is no longer possible, the treaty is no longer in force.

3. **Custom:** A consistent pattern of practice by states that is deemed to constitute an international law.

 a. Once established, customary international law is binding on all states in the international system, including those that do not practice it.

 b. Elements of custom:

  i. Material fact: The practice of states.

  ii. Duration: The reiteration of the practice over time.

  iii. Opinio juris: Respect for the custom out of a sense of legal obligation.

B. Laws of War are the rules that regulate both the recourse to war and military conduct in time of war.

1. *Jus ad bellum* rules regulate the right of states to go to war.

2. According to the United Nations Charter, states may only go to war for three reasons:

 a. **Self-defense:** The act of repelling an attack by another state.

 b. **Collective self-defense:** Assisting another state that has been attacked.

 c. **Security Council authorization:** Responding to a United Nations call to respond to an attack against a UN member state

3. *Jus in bello* rules regulate the conduct of armies in time of war. Key principles include:

 a. **Proportionality:** Using a level of military force in proportion to what is necessary to achieve limited objectives.

 b. **Unnecessary suffering:** Using weapons of war and tactics that do not cause undue or unnecessary suffering.

 c. **Discrimination:** Differentiating between military and civilian actions.

C. Human Rights Laws are the rules that protect individual freedoms and liberties. Cornerstone human rights treaties include:

1. 1948 Universal Declaration of Human Rights
2. 1948 Genocide Convention
3. 1965 Convention on the Elimination of All Forms of Racial Discrimination
4. 1966 UN Covenant for Civil and Political Rights
5. 1966 UN Covenant for Social, Cultural and Economic Rights
6. 1967 Convention on the Elimination of All Forms of Discrimination Against Women
7. 1984 Convention Against Torture
8. 1989 Convention on the Rights of the Child

SOVIET MISSILES IN CUBA - 1962

↓ Surface to Air Missile (SAM) sites
↓ Surface to Surface Missile(SSM) sites
↓ Medium Range Ballistic Missile (MRBM) sites

International Political Economy

The interaction between political and economic forces in world politics.

A. Economic Theories

1. **Capitalism:** An economic system that emphasizes money, market-oriented trade and capital investment for further production and profit. Key elements:

 a. Minimal government intervention in economic affairs
 b. Supply and demand determine production and prices
 c. Free movement of service, money and people to maximize profits

2. **Mercantilism:** An economic system that emphasizes the accumulation of wealth. Key elements:

 a. Active government management of economic affairs
 b. Protectionism against foreign imports
 c. Promotion of trade surpluses through aggressive exports

B. Economic Division of States

1. **First World:** Wealthy states of Western Europe and North America.

 a. Capitalist
 b. Industrialized
 c. Sophisticated economic systems
 d. Citizenship with high per-capita incomes and long life expectancies

2. **Third World:** States of Asia, Africa and Latin America.

 a. Various non-capitalist economic systems
 b. Non-industrialized
 c. Exportation of raw materials
 d. Impoverished citizenry

3. **Economies in Transition:** States of Eastern Europe making the transition from controlled economies to market economies.

4. **Asian NICs:** Newly Industrialized Countries of East Asia.

C. International Economic Institutions

1. **International Monetary Fund (IMF):** Institution that provides short-term economic assistance to states experiencing economic troubles. States borrowing more than their allowed quota are required to adopt IMF conditions, which may include:

 a. Selling of state-owned industries and assets
 b. Lower government expenditures on public services
 c. Increased interest rates to prevent currency collapse
 d. Increased taxes

2. **International Bank of Reconstruction and Development (World Bank):** Institution that provides low-interest long-term loans to developing countries for infrastructure development. Typical World Bank projects include:

 a. Roads
 b. Bridges
 c. Dams
 d. Sea ports
 e. Communications systems

3. **General Agreement on Tariffs and Trade (GATT):** Series of multilateral agreements designed to coordinate the reduction of tariffs on imports. GATT rounds include:

 a. Geneva, Switzerland (1947-1948): 23 participating states
 b. Annecy, France (1948-1949): 33 participating states
 c. Torquay, England (1950-1951): 34 participating states
 d. Geneva, Switzerland (1955-1956): 22 participating states
 e. Dillon Round (1960-1962): 45 participating states
 f. Kennedy Round (1964-1967): 48 participating states
 g. Tokyo Round (1973-1979): 99 participating states
 h. Uruguay Round (1986-1994): 125 participating states

4. **World Trade Organization (WTO):** Institution created in 1995 to replace the GATT. The WTO is empowered to both adjust international trade rules and settle conflicts arising over their interpretation.

WTO meeting in Doha, Qatar 2001

United Nations

A. The United Nations (UN) was created in 1945 in the aftermath of the Second World War to promote international peace, security, economic development and social justice.

1. Headquartered in New York City, the UN is open to all nations and in 2001 had a membership of 189 states.

2. The UN's Charter created the organization and outlines its procedures and powers.

B. Principal organs of the United Nations:

1. **General Assembly (GA):** Open to all United Nations members, the General Assembly passes resolutions that address any issue on its agenda. General Assembly resolutions, passed by a simple majority of voting members, are non-binding, reflecting international opinion.

2. **Security Council (SC):** The United Nations organ responsible for the maintenance of international peace and security. Security Council resolutions are legally binding. For a resolution to pass in the Security Council it must pass two tests:

 a. Super-majority (9 of 15) vote
 b. Concurring votes of the five permanent members

C. Membership is reserved to 15 states.

1. **Permanent members (P5):** Five states (China, France, Russia United Kingdom, United States) always present on the Security Council that enjoy a veto power on all substantive resolutions.

2. **Rotating members (R10):** 10 states selected on a regional basis that serve for two-year terms.

3. **The Security Council** is empowered to authorize peacekeeping operations (PKOs) in response to threats to international peace and security. Peacekeeping operations are multinational forces that operate under the United Nations flag.

D. Economic and Social Council (ECOSOC): Composed of 54 UN members, ECOSOC considers issues relating to:

1. Standards of living
2. Economic and social development
3. Health-related problems
4. International cultural and educational cooperation
5. Universal respect for human rights and fundamental freedoms

E. Trusteeship Council: UN organ responsible for the transition of trust territories to independent states. The 11th, and final, trust territory of Palau was admitted as a member of the United Nations in 1994, exhausting the Trusteeship Council's agenda.

F. International Court of Justice (ICJ):

1. Located in The Hague, Netherlands, the ICJ is the principal judicial organ of the United Nations.

2. The ICJ's 15 judges rule on cases brought before it by states. The ICJ also renders advisory opinions to the General Assembly and Security Council when requested.

G. Secretariat: The administrative staff that serves the United Nations and its member-states.

1. The highest office in the Secretariat is held by the **Secretary-General,** who is elected for five-year renewable terms by the General Assembly and Security Council.

2. Secretaries-General:

 a. Trygve Lie, Norway, 1946-1953
 b. Dag Hammarskjold, Sweden, 1953-1961
 c. U Thant, Burma, 1961-1971
 d. Kurt Waldheim, Austria, 1971-1981
 e. Javier Perez de Cuellar, Peru, 1981-1991
 f. Boutros-Boutros Ghali, Egypt, 1992-1996
 g. Kofi Annan, Ghana, 1997-

United Nations Headquarters in New York City

Arms Control

The negotiated regulation of military weapons.

A. Categories of arms control:

1. **Arms reduction:** Agreement that results in an overall decrease in the number of weapons.

2. **Arms freeze:** Agreement to halt the production of weapons.

3. **Arms limitation:** Agreement to limit the number or type of weapon to a specific level.

B. Major nuclear arms control accords:

1. 1963 Limited Test Ban Treaty (LTBT)
2. 1970 Nuclear Non-Proliferation Treaty (NPT)
3. 1972 Anti-Ballistic Missile Treaty (ABM)
4. 1972 Strategic Arms Limitation Talks (SALT)
5. 1979 Strategic Arms Limitation Talks (SALT II)
6. 1987 Intermediate-Range Nuclear Force Treaty (INF)
7. 1991 Strategic Arms Reduction Treaty (START)
8. 1996 Comprehensive Test Ban Treaty (CTBT)
9. 1993 Strategic Arms Reduction Treaty (START II)
10. 1997 Strategic Arms Reduction Treaty (START III)

Actors in World Politics

A. States are geographic entities governed by a central authority, whose leaders claim to represent all persons within the territory. The emergence of states at the turn of the 16th century ushered in the modern international system.

1. Elements of a state:

 a. **Territory:** Includes the surface area and beneath to the core of the Earth, twelve miles of adjacent sea and the airspace above the land and territorial sea.
 b. **Population:** Citizens of the state.
 c. **Government:** Central controlling political institutions.
 d. **Recognition:** Formal declaration from other states that an entity is a state.

2. Categories of states:

 a. **Hegemon:** Dominant state that writes and enforces international rules.
 b. **Great power:** State that defines its interests globally, wins most of the wars that it fights and participates in the major international diplomatic conferences.
 c. **Minor power:** State with little international influence that defines its interests narrowly.

B. International Organizations (IOs) are multilateral institutions created by states in order to pursue common objectives that cannot be achieved unilaterally. International organizations emerged as a major component of the international landscape during the twentieth century.

C. Transnational Non-governmental Organizations (NGOs): Institutions composed of private, non-state international actors, such as individuals, that cut across national boundaries.

WAR

A. War: A conflict carried on by force of arms, as between states or between parties within a state.

1. **International war:** A war involving two or more states.

2. **Civil war:** War taking place between parties within a state.

3. Political scientists have established a minimum battle death threshold of 1,000 to differentiate war from conflict short of war.

B. Wars have both **immediate** and **underlying** causes.

1. An **immediate cause** is an event that occurs just prior to the onset of war that is considered the point of no return.

2. **Underlying causes,** long-term trends that take place years or decades prior to the onset of the war, condition states and the international system for war.

C. Categories of war:

1. **Systemic War** involves most, if not all, great powers in a prolonged and particularly destructive conflict over the structure of the international system.

 a. Systemic wars determine global leadership.
 b. Other terms used include **structural war, hegemonic war and world war.**
 c. Since 1500, there have been six systemic wars:

  i. Thirty Years' War (1618-1648)
  ii. War of the Spanish Succession (1701-1713)
  ii. Wars of the French Revolution (1792-1802)
  iv. Napoleonic Campaigns (1803-1815)
  v. World War I (1914-1918)
  vi. World War II (1939-1945)

2. **Great Power War** involves at least one great power on each side of the conflict. Since 1500, there have been sixty-four great power wars, the most recent was the Korean War (1950-1953) between the United States and China.

3. **Interstate War** is a conflict with one or more great powers fighting on one side against non-great powers on the other. More than 120 interstate wars have been fought since 1500.

4. **Minor Power** War is a conflict between two or more states, none of which is a great power.

5. **Civil War** is an internal struggle between parties from the same state. A civil war may be fought to determine the leadership of the state or to secure the independence of part of the state from the central government.

D. Levels of War:

1. **Nuclear war** involves the use of atomic, nuclear or thermonuclear weapons. The Pacific Theater of World War II became a nuclear war when the United States dropped atomic bombs on Hiroshima and Nagasaki in August 1945.

2. **Total war** is a conflict that affects and involves all segments of society, rather than solely the militaries of the participating states. World War I is widely viewed as history's first total war, with civilian casualties outnumbering battle deaths.

3. **High-Intensity Conflict (HIC)** is a general war that involves major weapons systems and substantial amounts of armed soldiers.

4. **Low-Intensity Conflict (LIC)** is an unconventional war fought in the Third World that is smaller in terms of military scale.